What readers say about *Wisdom from the Gardens*

"For those struggling to find an internal peace, this is a quiet book which guides us through the cycles of nature as a way to guide us through the cycles in our lives."
Dr. Aili Pogust, Educational Consultant, Coach and Trainer

"Wisdom from the Gardens – Life Lessons is a beautifully illustrated compact book full of themes anyone seeking balance of mind, body and spirit in today's world will find helpful."
Natasha Dachos, Social Worker

"Anyone seeking solace in the natural world will find comfort in the quiet, yet strong images that the author has created. Well done! A wonderful and calming experience!"
Dr. Nadine McHenry, Widener University

"In reading Wisdom from the Gardens, you accompany Mary Beth Ford as she reveals insights of life's lessons, seasoned by the blessings of nature. She transforms the reader from casual observer to active participant."
David Parkhurst Crane, Classical guitarist and *Grammy Award* candidate

"I would recommend this book to anyone who seriously desires a deeper spirituality in everyday life. The topics are so timely and the content so real."
Dr. Kathryn A. Miller, SSJ, Chestnut Hill College

"I was amazed by the clarity and sense of oneness that the author created for her reader. A must read for anyone who feels a connection between the natural world and the soul of humanity."
Rev. Jay Gullo, Spiritualist Minister and Metaphysical Counselor

Wisdom from the Gardens

Life Lessons

Mary Beth Ford, Ed.D.

Illustrations by Kimberlee S. Henson

INFINITY PUBLISHING

Copyright © 2005 by Mary Beth Ford, Ed.D.

ISBN 978-0-7414-6861-1 Paperback
ISBN 978-0-7414-9602-7 eBook

Printed in the United States of America

Second Printing

Published April 2013

INFINITY PUBLISHING
1094 New DeHaven Street, Suite 100
West Conshohocken, PA 19428-2713
Toll-free (877) BUY BOOK
Local Phone (610) 941-9999
Fax (610) 941-9959
Info@buybooksontheweb.com
www.buybooksontheweb.com

To Barry

With love and appreciation

Contents

Reflections on a Calling

I am going to broadcast the seed and let the wind carry it where it will.

Pierre Teilhard de Chardin

I've exchanged smiles with many people on my nature walks. I've noticed the thoughtful looks of those who sit quietly on garden benches. Different ages, different backgrounds. Yet somehow I know we are seekers together. We share a calling to discover our purpose for being on earth. I think of our common bond as I begin to write down my reflections. We are busy people wanting to live spirit-filled lives in a secular world. I've pondered this dilemma for a long time.

Life balance has eluded me since I was a teenager. My search for balance has taken a long, spiral path. Obstacles challenged me. Tranquil times allowed me to catch my breath and absorb my learning. I've gained much from reading books about other spiritual journeys. I've reflected on these stories and attempted to put my own experiences in perspective. Yet I struggle to listen more closely to my heart.

Perhaps the greatest challenge has been releasing my grip on the steering wheel of life. I've been a lonely traveler, charting my own way. Now I want to change. I ask for Divine guidance. I quiet my incessant thoughts and trust my deepest feelings. A need for space to breathe leads me back to nature.

As a child, I loved to spend time outside. The colors and sounds and mysteries of nature intrigued me. Most especially, gardens captured my attention. Now, years later, gardens have become my sanctuary and my teacher. Life lessons emerge. Marvelous images unfold before my eyes.

I'm a visual learner. I see my garden lessons as seeds planted deep within, needing protection and nourishment. They've grown into a spiritual blueprint that guides my daily living. For a long while I considered writing down this plan and putting forth my ideas to the world. Since I'm neither a naturalist nor a philosopher, I mounted strong resistance to the idea. What will my family and friends think? What credentials do I have other than the wisdom that comes from having lived this long? Yet an inner urge persists. It calls me to fulfill my dream.

I've always been fascinated by stories of the sacred covenant between writers, musicians, and artists with the Great Creator. Many described themselves as instruments through which the flow of ideas poured out on paper from a Higher Source. Inspired by their stories, I too undertake collaboration with my Creator. I gather courage to share the story of my own journey.

A friend introduced me to Hildegard of Bingen—a powerful teacher in my search for balance. Hildegard was a visionary, naturalist, playwright, poetess and composer whose presence is still felt around the world more than eight hundred years later. This remarkable woman has become my muse. Her love of nature and teaching about a creation-centered spirituality has inspired me. Hildegard described herself using such lovely imagery:

Listen, there was once a king sitting on his throne. Around him stood great and wonderfully beautiful columns ornamented with ivory, bearing the banners of the king with great honor. Then it pleased the king to raise a small feather from the ground and he commanded it to fly. The feather flew, not because of anything in itself but because the air bore it along. Thus am I a feather on the breath of God.

I feel a connection with Hildegard because she sought to illuminate the divine in nature through useful and practical ways. I share her concern for usefulness. I also want to help others who seek balance of body, mind, and spirit in a world of conflicting values. Hildegard hesitated in answering the call to write down her insights. She expressed feelings of inadequacy to begin public preaching and teaching at a later age. I understand her doubts. Hildegard inspires me to risk sharing my thoughts about life balance.

Anne Morrow Lindbergh's desire to think through her questions with paper and pencil in the solitude of an island retreat reflects my own way of grappling with life's meaning and purpose. I first read her *Gift from the Sea* many years ago. Its simple, yet profound, wisdom still resonates with me today. During summer vacations I have carried *Gift from the Sea* on trips to the beach. I've sat on a solitary rock in the early morning hours to ponder its wise counsel. This classic book captured so well the essence of my own struggle for balance.

I learned much from my reflections on the sea and its shells. But my questions about how to live in the world with Spirit persisted. I've always loved walks in gardens and began to record their images in a journal. They were only jottings at first. But as I reflected on the images, I saw connections with life. I knew the images themselves did not have meaning; still they resonated deep within me. Garden wisdom took root.

Anne Morrow Lindbergh drew her inspiration from the beach and the collection of shells that she found there. My inspiration has come from frequent walks in nature and quiet times in gardens. The wisdom drawn from these lovely places has touched my soul. It has nurtured the seeds of spiritual knowing deep within.

In the manner of Hildegard of Bingen I put aside all fears and doubts and begin my spiritual journey as a "feather on the breath of God." In the manner of Anne Morrow Lindbergh I draw on nature's images and share my wisdom from the gardens. I offer nature's lessons to all who ponder life's purpose and search for balance between world and Spirit.

INTRODUCTION

Harmony in the Gardens

Life had a certain rhythm to it for a decade or so. I ran as fast as I could all week. Then each Sunday morning I'd visit Longwood Gardens to quiet my mind and restore my inner balance. I breathed an audible sigh of relief as the magnificent Copper Beech Allee came into view. A palpable calm spread over my body. It was a precious time of renewal for me each week and one that passed by all too quickly.

Through time I have come to see these gardens— not as a collection of lovely flowers and majestic trees—but as a vibrant community. This revelation changed my perspective and shifted my search for balance in a crucial way. Now as I soak in nature's sights and sounds and smells, I use my senses to discover the fascinating web of diverse relationships that surround me. What lessons does nature teach if I choose to quiet my busy mind and pay close attention? The invitation entices me. I become nature's student and explore its wondrous harmony and diversity.

Viewing nature as a community has revealed an interdependence among diverse members that I had overlooked for many years. The ancient Greeks used the word *harmozein* to depict things that seem to fit together. Today's scientists describe nature as a complex, interconnected system that tends toward balance. They observe a system that remains stable and seems to resist change. They study the factors that break its stasis and necessitate a change. Nature's complexity means almost anything can happen. The natural world intrigues me.

On my nature walks, I pay close attention to the stresses that regularly occur. Hard weather, invasive species, and human negligence take their toll. I watch nature's resilience as it gradually recovers from each event. I wonder about nature's tendency toward balance, yet resistance to change. I make connections between what I observe in nature and what I know about life.

Nature's mysterious drive to actively maintain its stasis makes me reflect on my own desire for balance. We are part of this same complex, interconnected, chaotic system. Our lives do not evolve from A to Z in a nice, neat fashion. Detours pull us off balance. Often we struggle to adjust. And as we do, a mysterious voice from deep within calls us back to center.

But we don't always listen to this call. Many of us avoid change until our lives become intolerable. Even then we resist, sometimes for years. Where do we get stuck and why? What makes us wake up and rethink our lives? Our marriages? Our careers? What breaks our resistance and moves us toward growth and renewal?

For me, change happens when joy evaporates from the inside out. I feel brittle and find life no longer works. Finally I let go. I surrender my will and accept Spirit's mysterious call to search for the way home. As I deepen my connection to Spirit, my inner and outer worlds transform.

Through my struggle for life balance, I learn compassion for others and the world. But I must be whole within before I can honor my bond with all creation. Only when I learn reverence for my inner Spirit can I reach out with compassion to help others. Creation at its core is about balance and relationship.

The natural world reminds us that relationships are wondrously varied and complex. Through nature's diversity, we can observe some cooperation and some competition. Living things compete or cooperate to survive within an environment of limited resources. But we cannot look for parallels to resolve our life questions. The answers lie deep within us, waiting to be discovered. Still the natural world offers us some wisdom about cooperation and competition within relationship.

I observe the butterfly and the blossom. Cooperation must directly benefit each member's efforts to succeed. Both need one another to flourish; both benefit from the exchange. I learn that giving and receiving are one, different aspects of the same Life Force. Sometimes the universe seems to dictate a law of sacrifice for the sake of future generations.

I watch a spider capture its prey as a means of sustaining life. Spiders help to control pest insects that wreak havoc in any garden. But they will just as happily consume a lovely butterfly. As I witness garden predators in action, I must confront the presence of competition in relationship.

Bird feeders in winter provide a perfect place to observe competition in action. Snow falls and food becomes scarce. Tiny birds twitter about, snatching bits of seed and flying nearby to enjoy them. Occasionally larger birds will intrude and take over. The small birds retreat and watch for an opportunity to sneak back. Then we have the ingenious squirrels. They often figure out ways to thwart a squirrel-proof device and take over an area. This dance of competitors around a bird feeder allows each creature's best traits to flourish. But how does beneficial competition turn destructive? The story of kudzu can offer us some insights. Kudzu is an ornamental plant, native to China and Japan. It has large leaves and sweet-smelling blooms. Ground kudzu has been used for centuries in foods and medicines. In recent times, however, kudzu has been transplanted to new environments without any natural insect enemies. Its vines have become invasive, keeping out the light and destroying valuable forests. Depending on its use, kudzu can be either beneficial or destructive.

Human competition also has two sides. It intensifies our effort and sharpens our focus. But for what end? Loving service unites us in a worthy cause. War and hatred also create a common purpose. Remember the story of kudzu. Even the beneficial aspects of our lives can become invasive and keep the light from reaching our souls. When we stay close to the earth, we recover our sense of balance and make good choices. We remember our shared purpose with all creation.

In my role as nature's observer, I record descriptions of the partnerships and connections I witness during each season. The image of a vibrant garden community emerges—one that accommodates the many different species living within its borders. It thrives on this diversity. Each member nurtures the garden's growth and helps maintain its harmony. Each member's role is essential.

The garden community reveals that interdependence and diversity are the keys to its growth and harmony. It benefits from the open exchanges among its members. Nature offers us opportunities to study the different species that cooperate and share overlapping roles.

I've filled several journals with my observations and reflections. I've used an artist's sketch pad to draw comparisons between the gardens and life. I've outlined nature's teachings about oneness and diversity. My challenge now is to absorb these lessons. I reflect on how they can help resolve my struggle between world and Spirit.

From the world's viewpoint we live a lonely and isolated existence that requires us to compete for survival. Yet sacred wisdom traditions share the vision of a loving Creator, whose Divine Essence flows through all creation. Plants and flowers, trees and shrubs have nourished our sense of oneness with the universe for eons. We grow gardens in backyards and on balconies — put flowerpots on doorsteps and windowsills. Gardens mirror our connection with the cosmos. But gardens also reveal the dark side of nature. They remind us that uncertainty and loss are a part of the cosmic mysteries and a predicament for all life.

Times of crisis and tragedy complicate our lives. They break open our hearts and refocus our perspective. War and terrorism, poverty and starvation, my brother Joe's diagnosis with lung cancer — I walk numb through the gardens with such dismal thoughts. How do I reconcile them with my belief in a loving Creator? How do I resolve this paradox? Not easily I find. But the gardens soothe my spirit. They help me understand that rebirth is also part of the cosmic cycle.

As I continue to learn and my thoughts continue to evolve, I shed fears and false beliefs layer by layer. I pursue my inner calling with its joys and challenges. I invite other seekers to join my garden walks in each season. Ponder with me nature's lessons on harmony.

Through the years these lessons have evolved into a blueprint for restoring balance and relationship to the center of life.

CHAPTER ONE

A Blueprint for Balance

uring many nature walks I've brought my questions about life's purpose and my search for balance between world and Spirit. My journal contains my musings. Through them I catch a glimpse of my Creator. I discover that nature offers us powerful images as reminders that we're not alone in our journey through life.

Early spring has arrived in the Gardens. Pansies, nestled under a cover of pine needles and winter snows, have begun to bloom once more with the early spring sun. Yellow winter aconites and lavender crocuses blanket the lawn on Oak Knoll in a carpet of color. Hyacinth and tulip bulbs emerge on the Flower Garden Walk. Hints of yellow burst forth on the witch-hazel bushes and on the weeping willow trees down by the lake. Birds delight me with their distinctive melodies. Squirrels frolic and chase one another, and geese have begun their spring mating ritual. Nature's unfolding brings such joy and contentment after the long winter hibernation. I witness the awesome power of the Universal Life Force re-creating the world before my eyes. I watch the diverse garden residents participating in this creative process.

The world's wisdom traditions teach us that a Divine Essence flows through all creation. Once we accept this truth, then it follows that we are one. We belong to the web of life. From belief in our unity flows appreciation for the incredible diversity of the universe. Such diversity within a garden community nurtures its growth and balance. Diversity within the human family promotes abundance and harmony in the world. Each member of a garden community has a necessary role in creating its oneness. Each one of us has a life purpose to collaborate with our Creator. Whatever work we do to use our talents, we each have a part to fulfill that is essential for the world's renewal and for our own happiness. This shared purpose unites us. It makes each one of us equally responsible to the whole of creation.

Oneness and diversity, special roles and shared purpose. A glimpse of these truths has become my treasured wisdom from the gardens. Keats said, "Beauty is truth, truth beauty." Perhaps our Creator intended nature's beauty as a catalyst for our meditation and learning, not just our admiration. Nature helps us connect with our spiritual power, our soul strength. We must be whole within ourselves in order to be most effective in the world. We must respect our own uniqueness in order to reverence the bond we share with others. My blueprint for balance offers a way to approach nature with focus and intention. Balance deals with choices. My choice to honor the Divine Presence in nature has changed how I see myself and how I live my life.

A sense of my oneness with nature has helped me to understand and accept that I am the Universal Life Force within. Slowly I'm allowing this Life Force to work in me and through me. I say slowly because it takes a while for such knowing to move from the head to the heart. Accepting the role of co-creator takes courage. It requires me to be fully aware of my profound connection with a Higher Power. It requires courage to say yes to partnership with my Creator and accept the responsibility this role demands.

Hildegard of Bingen, a medieval mystic of diverse gifts, had a passionate concern with the role of men and women as co-creators. She taught that we're called to cooperate actively with God in the perfection of creation. She wrote about a rational soul inserted in the body that it might guide the body in its way of living. In return, the body may contemplate the soul through faith. Hildegard first awakened in me a desire to explore my role as co-creator with my true Self.

An awareness of our partnership allows us to use our spiritual power wisely in daily life. Through this partnership we gain wisdom to guide our undertakings and learn from our mistakes. Struggles, fears, and anxieties signal our attempts to go it alone. They are truly blessings in disguise. They remind us to look within for strength and guidance. As Hildegard declared so passionately over eight hundred years ago, we have Spirit within sharing our purpose as co-creator in the world's renewal.

I've chosen the Lantana tree as a garden image to nurture my role as co-creator. Gardeners start with a small Lantana plant and prune it back to one stem. I see myself in this small plant. They tie the main stem to a stake to grow vertically. I envision my Sacred Self, supporting my small self to grow. Once the desired height is reached, gardeners pinch the tip of the stem to promote branching. They support the tree's trunk with a stake. The tree produces fragrant and colorful blossoms that delight visitors and butterflies alike. I have the support of my true Self as I grow and branch out through my writing. I share the balm of my garden wisdom with others.

The Lantana's image reminds me that I am never alone. I remember that the power of a loving Life Force flows through the small Lantana plant, through the specially created Lantana tree, and through me. When news reports make me anxious and fearful, this lovely image helps me regain hope for the world's renewal.

We have arrived at a crossroads as we begin the 21st century and a new millennium. The major problems of our time—poverty, overpopulation, violence and acts of terror, environmental degradation, extinction of plant and animal species—are systemic problems that cannot be solved in isolation. Their solutions require a change in values. We must understand that our actions affect generations to come and the whole of creation, as well as ourselves. Our choices now create our future.

The garden community demonstrates so clearly the effects of disharmony among its members. An invasive species takes over an area; too many deer browse at shrub level. Any imbalance in relationships lessens diversity. And loss of diversity affects the whole of creation.

In both natural and human worlds interdependence is the basis for all relationships. Each member has a unique role that fulfills its purpose. Each member's power to create or to destroy affects the harmony of the entire system. Modern science now confirms what mystics through the ages have told us. Everything in the universe is connected with everything else.

It's time that we see the universe as an integrated whole and feel our connection to this whole. It's time that we honor our sense of oneness that is at the heart of being fully human and spiritually aware. We heal from within. But our search for balance must expand beyond a desire for personal fulfillment. It must include commitment toward the world community.

We know that our efforts and determination to solve the world's problems call forth the power of the universe. We remember that we are spiritual beings in human form on this earth plane for our own learning and the world's renewal. As co-creators we have a calling to lead lives that reflect this grand purpose. Acceptance of our purpose draws the wisdom of our Creator into all we think and say and do. It offers us the balance and peace of mind we so earnestly seek.

But it's easy to lose our bearings in the midst of everyday living and find that we're without focus or balance. My brother Joe told me that facing his death changed his perspective on life. He fought to live with great courage and determination and a desire to enjoy whatever time he had left. Yet he accepted his death with the many fears and unknowns surrounding it with the same heroic spirit. Once we accept dying as a part of living, we can respond to each moment with appreciation. We are free to embrace life fully.

From my brother I've learned that the process for dying well is the same process for living well. From my garden images I've recreated my life through remembrance of my Divine Source. A balanced life means that I must nourish my whole self, as well as contribute to other people's lives and the world.

Life balance requires wisdom. By asking daily for the gift of inner sight, we stay secure in our purpose for living and our place in the universe. We recognize the sacred space within where Self and Creator unite in each present moment.

CHAPTER TWO

The Power of the Present Moment

 arden walks in summer are like walks through Monet's paintings. The beauty amazes me and allows me to ponder the Divine Presence on earth. I love to visit water lily ponds in late summer and imagine myself in Monet's gardens at Giverny. The water lily is my birth flower. I sit under a magnificent Copper Beech—one that I've adopted as my writing tree—and mull over ideas for my next chapter. I think of a quote from Shakespeare's *As You Like It:* "Tongues in trees, books in running brooks, sermons in stones, and good in everything." Nature is an eloquent teacher, providing her students

with powerful learning experiences of the here and now.

Several events from the past come to mind as moments of heightened awareness and gifts from nature. I was visiting my mother in the hospital after her release from a week's stay in intensive care and the day before she was due to go home. Mom was in a jubilant mood. She suggested that we walk down to the solarium and enjoy the sunset. As Mom soaked in the glorious display of colors, her face reflected the sky's beauty. Tears filled her eyes. Her deep emotion overwhelmed me.

During the early morning hours my mother's heart stopped beating. Nurses brought her back to life, but she slipped into a coma and died several days later. My mother's joyful response to her final sunset remains forever etched in my memory. In her face I saw awareness and appreciation for the gift of the present moment.

I had a similar experience while visiting family in Phoenix with my husband. We were touring Sedona and went up to see a lovely chapel built into a rock face on the mountainside. The wall behind the altar—solid glass from floor to ceiling—provided a mural image of the distant mountains to inspire those who had come to pray. I sat in the pew and gazed upon this awesome scene. Tears streamed down my face in this moment of communion with my Creator. I remembered my mother's sunset.

Yet another mountain offered me gifts of the moment, but in a much different way. My husband and I were hiking a trail on Vermont's Mount Mansfield. We came to a cliff that we would need to conquer in order to reach the top. As we stood discussing our options, a family with a young boy and a small dog came bounding down and continued on their way. Not to be outdone, we decided to go straight up the cliff, rather than take a longer and less strenuous route to the summit. We had climbed about half way, carefully selecting niches to place hands and feet, when Barry warned me not to look down. Glancing over my shoulder, I froze with fear. My mind did not wander as we finished our ascent and reached the top. We hugged one another in relief. Then we celebrated our triumph.

In my climb up the rock face, I found my concern with past and future recede and my awareness of the present heighten. I did not reflect on the problem before me and its meaning for my life. Despite my fear, I remained very still inside and focused in the present. I concentrated on one step—one moment at a time—like a series of still pictures running through a projector. The images from this experience remain.

My mother's final sunset, meditation in a mountain chapel, and my climb up a rock face—I treasure these memories of vivid awareness. They help me remember how it feels to be fully present. I ask my Inner Guide for the grace to live each day with such mindfulness.

The magic of the here and now allows each experience to displace thoughts of worry, guilt and regret. Such awareness enhances our enjoyment and nurtures our Spirit. Living in the now also helps strengthen our relationships. It develops our ability to be a true listener, rather than just a good listener. True listening requires a quiet, open mind—one that is respectful and loving. We remind ourselves that we have an opportunity to learn from a different perspective. We gain a feeling of personal connection. St. Benedict counsels us: "Listen and attend with the ear of your heart." Present moment awareness connects us with our deepest emotions. It increases our appreciation for small things that otherwise pass by unnoticed. We learn to pay attention to what's inside us as well as what's around us. Spending time in nature offers us wonderful practice for improving our ability to pay attention. Inner turmoil subsides. We focus our senses on sights and sounds and smells, enjoying our role as observer.

During the summer I'm often drawn to visit the beautiful Rosa 'Andeli' or "Double Delight" tea rose. I have a ritual for the occasion. First I circle the bush slowly and admire the flower's colorful red blend with its white center. Then I notice the long stems and long, narrow flower buds. Several blossoms attract my attention with their particular beauty and beckon me to inhale their fragrance. Such loveliness and perfume are a double delight. I finish my ritual with a whispered prayer of thanks for the joys of creation. I feel blessed.

Expressing appreciation is a way of staying anchored in the now. The Divine Presence is always around us and within us. Removing blocks to awareness and appreciation of our Life Force requires choice, commitment and practice. At times crisis and loss accelerate our learning. Through our pain we reach out to our Creator and regain our reverence and appreciation for life itself.

During his last year on earth my brother Joe was known as a thankful person. Facing his death made him more open to what is — more determined to savor each moment he had left. He expressed his thanks for the smallest joy or help given him. Through my

brother's example I find myself growing in appreciation for life's simple pleasures that I once took for
granted. As I learn to anchor myself in the present, I
find time holds me captive less often.

Poets describe us as prisoners of time and declare
that time is our nemesis. If we listen carefully to our
language, we will know that this is true. Quantity
seems to be the essence of time. Experts warn us not to
waste time. Time is money. Clocks and calendars
measure the march of time. Our scheduling books
overflow with dates, deadlines and things to do. We
value speed and efficiency above all. But over activity
and obsession with time threaten our inner life and
peaceful mind. We want to have time as our friend. We
must reconnect with its deeper meaning.

By observing the rhythms of time in nature—the
sun's path across the sky, the growth of seeds, the
changing seasons—we realize that time is not a
mechanical measure. It measures process. By detaching
from clock time for even a short while, we can allow
ourselves some moments of sanctified laziness. We
grow to appreciate time's fullness in the process. Time
becomes our friend.

The power of the present moment helps you remember the Life Force within that is your true Self.
Disconnect from your Life Force leads to a discon-
nected way of living. Claiming the power of your true
Self offers a life of balance between world and Spirit.
You can ask your Self frequently during the day: Am I
shining forth who I really am? Is this what I really want
to be doing? Guidance always comes, often in
unexpected ways.

Decisions may seem complex, but this is a smoke
screen of resistance you put forth. A choice is either for

Spirit or away from Spirit. Your mind will distract and discourage you. But your Spirit needs only a small opening of willingness to restore wholeness and inner peace. True humility recognizes Spirit within as a spark of the Divine Intelligence, while the world seeks to prove this as arrogance. Each moment presents an opportunity for choice. Each choice states the value you place on yourself. The plan is simple. Follow your heart's desire. Choose to honor Spirit within through your worldly existence.

I've spent many years searching for ways to develop a relationship with my Sacred Self and maintain balance between world and Spirit. I ask often for guidance to see, hear, feel and know what is true. By humbly asking to connect with Spirit, I've begun to reclaim time for myself. I'm discovering the power of living in the present.

Full attention to the present moment is the most prayerful response we can make for the gift of life and the greatest gift we can give another. In return for our commitment we receive blessings beyond measure. We have increased awareness of other persons, our surroundings and our impact in the world. We have clear vision about who we really are and what life can offer us. Each present moment connects us with our Creator and all of creation. Each present moment offers us guidance and protection, power and strength to fulfill our role as co-creators. Each present moment restores our balance between world and Spirit.

Being in the moment allows us to suspend judgment and trust Spirit guidance, while the world sees this approach as foolish and chaotic. Letting go of judgment allows our loving Self to shine forth, while disconnect from Spirit creates distance from our Life

Source. We strive for worldly goods and honors, rather than accept the Divine glory within us for which no striving is necessary. We define our needs based on the world's values, rather than listen to the desires of our heart.

We can persist in cluttering our minds with worldly goals that preoccupy us on a daily basis. We can persist in squeezing Spirit out of our lives. But sooner or later we'll come face to face with the emptiness of our existence. As Hildegard of Bingen counseled us over eight hundred years ago:

Like billowing clouds,
Like the incessant gurgling of the brook,
The longing of the Spirit can never be stilled.

Nature, more than anything else, deepens my experience of the Divine. It offers me a sense of expansion beyond my ordinary self.

On a sultry summer day I stroll down the Flower Walk, enthralled by the hundreds of butterflies clustered around the Lantana trees. I focus on one particular butterfly—a tiger swallowtail—and study its deep yellow wings with their black edges and black stripes. I watch my particular butterfly select certain blossoms to savor and bypass others. The selection process intrigues me. Those of us who linger nearby feel like honored guests at a banquet.

The lovely butterfly helps me practice stepping forth from the prison of my mind into the sacredness of the present moment. I breathe deeply and focus. Breathing brings me back to center. Focusing reconnects me with my Life Force. I learn to string these present moments together into a meditation. My quiet times in nature allow sacred space in which to nurture my true Self and my creative expression.

CHAPTER THREE

The Need for Solitude

n a rock jetty at the Jersey shore I sat quietly and savored the early morning hours of my summer vacation days. I was in my thirties at the time. The scent of the salt air, the lapping of the ocean against the rocks, the rays of the sun glistening on the water calmed and restored my Spirit. I longed for more frequent times of stillness to catch my breath. Now here I am, years later, sitting under my favorite Copper Beech, still grappling with the same issues. The need for quiet space and time that confronted me in my youth persists.

Finding time alone presents itself first and foremost. But this challenge is only the tip of the iceberg. Once I've created a space of peace and quiet, how do I still my mind so that I don't fritter the time away with random thoughts? What can I do each day to fulfill my inner needs? How do I balance the outer pressures of my world with the inner desires of my Spirit? What have I learned?

We seek many things in this world to bring us happiness and increase self-worth in our own eyes. But these things actually limit us and restrict awareness of our true Self. We fear losing our status and our possessions. We set goals for ourselves and struggle to accomplish them, while the sands of time shift beneath our feet. Daily stresses and responsibilities create what seem like insurmountable obstacles to a peaceful solitude. We are restless. Yet we refuse to acknowledge the desires of our Spirit.

The world's wisdom traditions tell us that we need solitude to know our Divine Source. We must take time to slip away from the world and renew the inner Self. We dry up and grow brittle when we ignore the needs of Spirit. The more we esteem the things of this world, the more we will perceive them as essential for our happiness. Through our determination, we can free ourselves from this prison that we've created. But we need quiet to hear our inner voice and receive guidance. How can we expect wisdom from within if we're never still enough to listen?

Only in solitude can we know our deepest thoughts and feelings. I resolve to preserve time in each day to meet this need for stillness. I renew my efforts daily to create a center of peace within.

I've learned that nothing outside myself can give me peace or disturb my peace. No person, no situation or event, no possession has this power. Peace is an inside job.

I alone am responsible for my life—for my thoughts, words and actions.

Then I must accept responsibility to create space in each day to nourish my Inner Spirit. I have tried different approaches. The ones that work best for me are actually quite simple.

I spend the first few minutes of each morning in prayer, asking my true Self for guidance. What would you have me say and do today? I pray for wisdom. Help me, Sacred Self, to see as you see, hear as you hear, feel as you feel, know as you know. Each evening I spend the last few minutes in a prayer of appreciation for the day's blessings and a prayer of forgiveness for my failings. My morning prayer helps me stay grounded in the present moment. My evening prayer gives my day closure before I sleep. These rituals sustain me.

Creating sacred space for solitude is another story. I can't say that I've found an easy answer, but I do have a strategy that works most of the time. I've set for myself what I call "Bottom Lines." Physical exercise, time for Spirit and my writing have become integral parts of each week. All other activities must fit in the remaining time or wait for another day. As a result, I'm not as efficient as I once was, but I am more peaceful. Since life is often unpredictable, I've promised myself that I will omit my "Bottom Lines" only when my heart pulls me in another direction. Planning for peace and not pressure has become my guiding principle.

The challenge of how to care for the soul in the midst of life's busyness requires an individual solution. Simply put: What do you enjoy doing that quiets your mind and feeds your creative center? Among my favorites are hiking, playing the piano, reading, and writing in my journal.

I used to see these activities as luxuries in my life. I felt guilty when I strayed from more "productive" work to pursue them. I've learned how foolish and destructive this way of thinking is. I realize now that what matters is paying attention to my inner needs for a while. Time alone renews us.

In solitude we can begin to decipher our life purpose and the special gifts we have come to share with the world community. Solitude allows us to release from ego and move beyond self. It is a quiet place where dreams begin. Solitude is our time with Spirit. It is a way to keep our center balanced and loving. With too much activity we even forget this sacred space is there.

A walk in nature stills my soul as nothing else can. It offers me a chance to lose myself for a brief period of time and connect with the rhythms of the universe. I walk in the Gardens when my heart is bursting with joy and gratitude. I walk in the Gardens when my heart is breaking with pain and sadness.

September 11, the day of the terrorist attacks, was one such occasion when my husband Barry and I took refuge. As we made our way near the Italian Water Gardens, we were amazed to see a double rainbow reflected in the spray of the fountains. The sight awed us. It was as if nature understood our emotions and offered us an eloquent message of hope. Several weeks later I learned of my brother Joe's diagnosis with inoperable lung cancer. My world fell apart again. Once more I retreated to nature for comfort and healing.

Through the years I've developed an affinity for old trees and an appreciation for their power to inspire. Old trees have sturdy root systems burrowed deep into the ground. They've weathered many storms and wear their scars proudly. They remind us that ongoing creation is a difficult process. We too have our scars. But the old trees prompt us to celebrate these imperfections as signs of our healing and renewal.

I am drawn to sit under my Copper Beech friend by the Flower Walk and bring my questions: How do I encourage my brother's will to live and yet help him prepare for an early death? Why will one who has the will to live die young and one who has lost desire for life linger on? I visit the stately oak at the far edge of the Gardens—the one I call "Guardian of the Meadow"—and stand quietly beneath its branches. I whisper prayers for Joe in the presence of my tree friends. Somehow I sense their blessings for me and for my brother. The trees console me.

The woodland down by the lake has been developed as an art-form garden with various "rooms." My favorite space creates an outdoor cathedral with branches of tall trees for the ceiling, tree trunks for the columns, native rhododendrons and azaleas at the far edge for the walls. Ground cover provides a carpet, birds supply the music, and flowering understory trees serve as the decorative art. During fall sunlight streams through branches on changing leaves and creates the effect of stained glass windows. Visitors to the cathedral have comfortable pews—wooden benches scattered throughout the woods— for times of solitude and meditation. Plants produce nature's incense to calm the mind and soothe the spirit. I sit in my private pew. I feel the Divine Presence around me and offer a prayer of thanks for the gift of this sacred place and moment.

We pay an enormous price for ignoring the needs of Spirit. Quiet periods bring us back in touch with who we really are. They help us see this truth in everyone around us. Quiet times heal the mind and restore us once again to bring peace into the world. We remember our life purpose. In stillness we receive wisdom to fulfill this purpose and grace to accept the peace that lies deep within.

Every significant spiritual tradition has offered meditation as a way of tapping the divine energies of love and wisdom. The practice of daily meditation creates a quiet space and time in which to know our true Self. It helps us integrate our personality with a Higher Power so that we can participate as co-creators in the world's renewal. Meditation should be enjoyable and not a grim duty. The heart of meditation is contentment in the now, fully aware of the Divine Presence within us and around us. Such awareness takes practice.

Fresh out of high school, I had my first experience with meditation as a novice in a religious order. We would rise at five each morning and make our way to the dark chapel for prayers and contemplation before Mass. Once again we would assemble in the late afternoon for the same spiritual exercises before supper. I mostly remember struggling with tiredness at those times. We helped one another keep awake with a prod to stand up. Once I had to keep from laughing aloud as the novice standing beside me pitched over the pew in her sleepy stupor. What a rocky start! But gradually I came to enjoy meditation practice as a time for reflection during the busy day.

After fourteen years I left my religious order and struggled to make a transition to the secular world. I felt incredible stress. Beginning a new life chapter, I searched for a job and a place to live, while making a whole new circle of friends. It never occurred to me that meditation could be a source of strength and wisdom as I charted each new direction. I simply did not consider making quiet time for reflection a priority, despite years of practice as a nun. I had not yet made a personal connection with my Creator. I had allowed meditation to be an intellectual process, rather than a spiritual practice.

There are many forms of meditation, each with its own adherents. I now believe that the real significance lies, not in our choice of form, but in our purpose. When we rest in the Divine Presence, we integrate our spiritual power into our self-expression. What matters is that we resolve to set time aside each day to honor and nurture Spirit.

Ten minutes has as much value as two hours if our purpose is clear. One does not need to live in a convent or monastery to practice effective meditation.

I suggest you create a quiet, sacred space in which to sit or lie down in a comfortable position. Bless your space and place in it objects that are important to you.

I find that certain rituals help put me in a meditative state. I've learned that my sense of smell has a powerful influence on my mood, so I always light a votive candle when I meditate. I play soft music. I've known for years the power of music to soothe and inspire me. The secret is to experiment with what appeals to your senses and helps you feel peaceful.

I've learned to pay attention to my breathing while I meditate. That spirit and inspiration both derive from the Latin word for breath is no coincidence. With eyes closed I focus on the Divine Presence that surrounds me. I follow my breath in and out. I feel my chest rise and fall. My body sinks into an oasis of light and peace. When random thoughts intrude, as they always do, I let them fade away and become background noise. For a few brief moments, my mind is actually clear of its chatter and open to Divine inspiration.

In the past few years I have begun the practice of what some call "open-eye" meditation—walks alone in natural surroundings. Several times each week I visit the Gardens for what I call my Spirit walks. Before beginning I remind myself that I can't receive gifts from nature if I don't pay close attention. I ask my Sacred Self for help. Where would you have me walk today? What would you have me learn? Sometimes I'll have a particular path in mind, only to find my way blocked for some reason. I used to become impatient. Now I just smile and wonder what surprise awaits me. Invariably, I find myself in a marvelous, unexpected place—just right for that moment.

There was a time when I considered solitude an impossible goal in a busy and active life. Solitude was a luxury I enjoyed during summer vacations, as if I could store up its benefits in some spiritual account for withdrawal during the rest of the year. Now I realize that only in solitude will I find the happiness and security I seek through so much busyness. Only in solitude will I discover the balanced center that I have desired for so long. Only in solitude will I develop the humility and courage to express my true Self in the world. My trust in Spirit grows.

CHAPTER FOUR

Learning to Trust

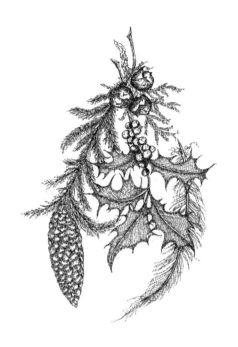

stensibly solid objects composed mainly of space fool the eye. Migratory birds know exactly when and where to return. I marvel at the mysteries of the universe. We are so different from each other, yet genetically we are quite similar. Our diverse bodily systems function together with such precision. I marvel at the mysteries of the human body. Pondering the unknowns of creation can be a stirring experience. Then why don't I regard the unknowns in my personal life with the same sense of awe and appreciation?

I understand that uncertainty is a predicament of life. There is a limit to my knowledge and my ability to foresee and control certain events and circumstances. The same questions continue to confound and haunt humankind. How can we live in this uncertain world without fear? How can we approach change, suffering and death with trust? Our lives are unpredictable and often chaotic. Our dread of the unknown persists. We struggle to see beauty and order beneath the seemingly random events of our lives.

Life faces us with our vulnerability on a daily basis. Western cause-and-effect thinking creates the illusion that we have the power to control our surroundings. We plan to leave nothing to chance. Chance is the enemy. But our attitude and actions eliminate opportunity for those experiences that transcend human limitations.

I've been an inveterate planner for my entire life, setting goals and ways to achieve them. I've acted as if I'm a solitary author, writing scripts of how my life should evolve. In recent years I've begun to find meaning in unexpected events. They've changed the direction of my life in ways I did not plan. I now recognize that times of crisis offer the potential for spiritual awakening and renewal, as well as for depression and despair. We have a choice.

The Chinese word for crisis has two symbols: one stands for danger, and the other, for opportunity. Our fears of the unknown signal danger and lead to isolation. We seek a safe haven and allow our fears to act as an anchor, holding us in place. I have behaved this way on too many occasions. If we trust in a loving Creator and draw strength from our oneness with all creation, then we gain courage to let go of our fears.

We accept the gift of unlimited opportunity. We understand that all people, events and circumstances are helpful for our growth. But how do I learn to trust at this deep level? How do I allow myself the certain wisdom of not knowing what to do? I take these questions to the Gardens during my Spirit walks. I wait patiently. I know the answers will come.

As I stroll in the Gardens during each season, I come to understand that the essence of life is change and mystery. A touch of sadness fills the air in late autumn as colorful leaves blanket the earth. The days grow shorter and colder. In late winter a lovely spring-like day follows on the path of a wicked snowstorm. Winter makes up its mind whether to stay or go. And such joy erupts a few weeks later as birds announce the return of warmth and light to the earth in a wild celebration of song. The seasons and their transitions give testimony. Nature, like life, has cycles of change and stability — some predictable and some unannounced.

Our life transitions follow the same pattern. Sometimes they signal a rite of passage, such as baptism or bat mitzvah. Sometimes they come unbidden, as mine did several years ago.

After working in various positions in the same public school district, I found myself transferred to the place where I had begun my employment. I was initially surprised but then delighted. This particular school had always been special to me. I loved the children and respected the faculty and parents here. Since the principal was retiring in two years, I saw my transfer as an unexpected opportunity to prepare myself and apply for the position.

I remember my first year back as one of the most joyful times in my career as an educator. I felt right at home and everything seemed to flow for me. But the second year did not go smoothly. I lost the principal's position and felt as if I had hit a brick wall. What did I do now? Where did I go? When life becomes as messy as mine did, one learns to recognize the hand of God behind the scenes.

Time in the Gardens has taught me to trust that each cycle passes. Change leads to stability, which sooner or later returns to change. Such is the rhythm of nature and such is the rhythm of life. A loving Creator has designed these cycles and natural rhythms to propel us forward.

I stayed in the district four more years, teaching second graders to delight in books and numbers and to form their signatures for the first time. I had not been in the classroom for many years. I had never taught children this young. But they offered me an oasis of joy and satisfaction, while I slowly detached from the work in which I had invested my entire adult life. I prepared to move on to where I did not know. It was a confusing and painful inner process.

Times of growth and change may last a short while or may take many years. In my transition from educator to writer, I needed space before I could settle down to put my thoughts on paper. My writing certainly brings me joy. But sometimes I feel as if I'm in exile, passing through a desert on my way to the Promised Land. I have a sense of not belonging anywhere — as if I'm in a cocoon waiting to emerge. I pray for patience.

In the Gardens I've observed that the process of change requires impermanence and patience that allows room for growth. Seeds, planted and nurtured by gardeners, must break open and grow in darkness for a fledgling plant to develop. Nature's rhythms depend on availability of resources and readiness to utilize them. Both seed and soul growth require proper conditions to flourish.

A spiritual journey requires patience and cannot be measured by a clock and a calendar but rather by lessons learned. I have discovered that writing this book has its own natural rhythm that I can't force. Sometimes I need to slow down and let the lessons simmer inside me for a while. Other times the ideas will pour forth at an amazing pace, often when I least expect them. I seem to learn the most when confusion and mystery overshadow my life.

Perhaps bulbs, more than any other planting, have helped me understand that mystery is at the heart of all growth. I've watched gardeners plant bulbs by the hundreds of thousands throughout the Gardens. Oak Knoll is my favorite site. On a sunny day in late winter, I spot there the first signs of bright yellow winter aconites and pale lavender crocuses peeking through the grass. By mid-March pools of color from Siberian squill and glory-of-the-snow will decorate the grassy hill. That the bulbs bloom at all is a miracle to me. They have lain dormant below the soil and survived the long, cold winter. Because the bulb is a food-storing structure, the plant is able to draw on this reserve supply and thrive despite the adverse conditions. Much of the growth and change from bulb to bloom takes place out of sight in a remarkable yet mysterious process.

Times of crisis, when our inner worlds turn dark and cold, offer us the opportunity for spiritual growth and transformation. Heaven asks us to face our deepest fears and learn endurance. We pray for the inner strength to make it through a difficult period, though prayer itself is often a struggle. Faith grows as we hang on, trusting that the crisis will end. Light will return once again to our lives. But many of life's problems seem to have no solution.

My brother Joe's illness with inoperable lung cancer is one such problem. Through diagnosis the doctors attempt to gain control and manage the uncertainty, but Joe's prognosis remains to be seen. His courage and determination in facing so many unknowns inspire me to learn from my brother's life. His pain and suffering require that I learn trust in a larger picture and humility to recognize what my human eyes can't see. In an effort to cope with my deep emotions, I find myself growing in appreciation each day for life's simple pleasures that I once took for granted. Giving thanks blesses us.

A walk in the Gardens during winter evokes my acceptance and appreciation for life just as it is. I am amazed that places of beauty can exist in a natural world turned brown and bare. A sense of wonder and mystery keeps me alert for the unexpected. By the entrance to the Eye of Water I notice the delicate red twigs of a Japanese maple glistening with droplets after a gentle winter rain. Along the Flower Walk I observe the red of a male cardinal, brilliant against a snowy backdrop, as it dines at the bird feeder. In Peirce's Woods the artistry of bare branches framed against a bright blue winter sky catches my eye. I appreciate the natural shape of each tree and notice high in the boughs large squirrel nests, revealed without their leafy camouflage. Why has this scene never struck me as beautiful before? Perhaps my favorite winter discovery has been a bench down by the lake surrounded by ordinary dried grasses. They hide me from the world and keep me warm on a cold winter's day. I pause here to reflect that nature, like life, has moments of beauty in the midst of bleak times.

From my reflections in the Gardens, I've discovered that having less control opens me to the possibility of new directions and more creative responses to life. My growing comfort in the presence of mystery helps me release my attachment to the known. Days of fear and doubt still come and go. But my lessening need for a particular outcome frees me from the specter of disappointment and failure. Each person in my life becomes a potential teacher. Each situation is a potential opportunity. When I succeed in staying connected to the present in this way, I feel more alive and aware. Being in the present moment does not interfere with my goal-setting and my desire for a certain direction. It simply keeps me alert to seize other opportunities.

In retrospect I realize that the loss of the principal's position, although painful to endure, was necessary to set me on a more comfortable life course. It offered me the opportunity to break out of what was once a good decision, but now no longer served me. I gradually came to honor my past choices, learn from them, and move on to make other choices. A loving Creator was asking me to beat my own drum, rather than dance to someone else's rhythm.

Once again I brought my questions to the Gardens during my Spirit walks. What is it that I really want to do? What ignites the fire within me? What sparks my greatest need to express myself? The response I received from within was a desire to write down my deepest thoughts and see where this path might lead me. I remembered Hildegard's image of a "feather on the breath of God" and let go of my fears. I was beginning a renewed search for what gives my life meaning. I was revitalizing my commitment to find life balance.

I have observed the Gardens as a living process in which everything plays a part in maintaining its harmony. Gardeners plant, water, fertilize and prune...nurturing the Life Force within. Colorful flowers have nectar that attracts bees to spread pollen. Birds of all sizes eat insects and keep their numbers under control. Frisky squirrels bury their nuts, some of which sprout as towering trees to provide shade and coolness. Each part is necessary—no part is too small—for producing the marvelous unity that I witness on my garden walks.

We also have a role in restoring the world's harmony. We are the voice of the Universal Life Force within. Without us this role will not be accomplished, this voice will not be heard. Each day holds gifts for us, but we must choose to accept them. Since the Divine way is full of paradoxes, our gift may involve suffering and pain for which there are no answers. But we're not alone.

It is yet another paradox that alone we can do nothing, but merged with our Sacred Self, we have spiritual power without limit. Too often, though, we create a careful persona to earn acceptance and admiration in the world's eyes. We hold onto what makes us miserable rather than risk a move into the unknown. When we fall out of rhythm with our true Self, we lose our balance and our way. When we sidestep fears to embrace our dream, we feel our lives flow with confidence. We return to balance. Our inner peace shows as we bless all those we meet with our smiles. We follow our heart's desire while faith in a loving Creator grows.

Nature teaches me to trust that Divine Intelligence understands and provides for my every need. I reflect on the Scripture admonition to observe the birds in the sky and the flowers in the field. Although birds neither sow nor reap and flowers neither work nor spin, I witness in nature how Divine Providence cares for their needs. Then why do I continue to worry about the future and doubt that such a loving Presence cares also for my well-being?

Nature chooses unusual ways to attract my attention and renew my wavering trust in the Divine Intelligence. During late winter gardeners set controlled brush fires in the meadow behind the Gardens to clear out the dead vegetation and stimulate new growth. It is fascinating to observe the burnt ground emerge into a meadow of purple and yellow wild flowers in the summer. Through this yearly ritual nature sends me a message. I must learn patience and endurance during those difficult times when my life's journey appears at a dead end. I must keep faith. Dark and barren periods actually provide the fertile loam in which new beginnings can germinate and take root.

On three separate occasions my true Self guided me to make radical decisions, change course and begin a new life. A period of struggle and resistance preceded each transition. The new direction made no sense to my logical mind. As a child and teenager, I managed responsibility beyond my years and had an excellent academic record. I was a social butterfly and loved dancing. At age eighteen I chose to leave behind the possibilities of college and enter a religious order. At age thirty I made the agonizing decision to leave my vocation as a nun. As a woman in the world—single for ten years and then happily married—I continued to work in education. Now my unrest and discontent were familiar signs. Another major change was coming.

The transition from educator to writer was the hardest one to accept because in many ways it was the most costly. I had invested thousands of dollars in degrees and certifications that were no longer useful to me. I lost pride each time someone questioned me about my future plans and I had no ready reply. I lost patience and became angry with myself for not being able to hold on to a secure position. But there was no room for maneuvering here. I was in a place that no longer served me. Had I stayed only for the money, I would have paid the highest cost of all with my physical and spiritual well-being.

During my life as a nun I lived without the world. During my life in education I lived without Spirit. Both lives kept me out of balance with my whole Self. I seek now to blend the learning from these two distinct worlds and unify them. I need to gather the wisdom from my years in the convent and my years as a teacher to complete what I had begun as a child and a teenager. None of the three phases was my whole expression. At present I feel like the bird in a cage that discovers how to pick the lock and desires to share its liberation. In writing this book I want to share that blueprint of learning with others and create an entirely new expression for myself in the process. Each day I ask my

Inner Spirit to show me what to do, where to go, and what to say for this purpose.

When I was a little girl, my parents taught me to pray before I got into bed and to ask a blessing on our meals. In school we'd bless the hour regularly—a lovely ritual as I look back. In the convent we had a particular regimen for morning and evening prayer with visits to the chapel after dinner and supper. I guess you could say that I've been immersed in prayer my whole life. And yet it is only in the past few years that I've felt the power of prayer at a deep level. I've learned to trust that a loving Creator understands my heart and interprets my prayers for the greatest good.

On the day Joe received his diagnosis of advanced lung cancer my family and I took refuge in prayer. Overwhelmed with emotion, we held hands around the kitchen table and prayed through our tears. We put our mother's memorial card on the table before us with its image of a child nestled in a sculpted hand along with the words of Isaiah: "See! I will not forget you. I have carved you on the palm of my hand."

We whispered our own words of comfort and love to Joe: "Remember you are always cared for. Remember you are never alone."

My brother's illness has provided me with an ongoing lesson in learning to trust Divine Providence. Often I question in my heart "Why Joe?" yet I know there is a larger purpose at work here that my small mind can't grasp. I search for what to say and how to help my brother, yet I know a Higher Power meets all his needs. I want to relieve Joe's pain and suffering, yet I know they have meaning for him in ways that are beyond my comprehension. I pray for guidance.

We are complicated beings, one day soaring high with hope and trust and the next day scraping bottom with doubts and fears. Hildegard of Bingen understood our vulnerability. She described us as "mud-bound Spirits" in her *Antiphon for Angels*. She urged us to shake off the weight of our worldly concerns and release our Spirits to fulfill their purpose for being on earth.

Hildegard struggled with her own feelings of inadequacy. She compared herself to a small feather raised from the ground by a powerful king who commanded her to fly "as a feather on the breath of God." This remarkable personality from the Middle Ages pursued her soul's passions with intensity, kept humble by the awareness that her creative powers arose from a Source within.

Hildegard inspires me to approach life with courage. She strengthens my faith in a loving Creator. I capture the glorious feeling of freedom and confidence that comes from learning to trust. I begin to live as a "feather on the breath of God." This deep trust allows me to shed my doubts and fears and to follow my dreams. Joy comes from Spirit. In the joy of my heart's desire I will find my balance.

CHAPTER FIVE

The Paradox of Love

od, the Universal Life Force, is love. The world's sacred traditions teach us this simple, yet powerful, truth. They declare that God's Life Force flows through us and makes us one with our Creator and with all creation. Then why do we often feel alone and adrift in the universe? Why do we judge harshly those with whom we share a deep, spiritual connection? When will we realize that our words and actions have a power to affect others beyond our imagining?

Each day we witness a world filled with angry, fearful people who often commit unspeakable atrocities towards one another. Grievances darken our perception of the world and separate us from our Source. They are alien to love, lead to confusion and guilt, and block Spirit guidance from within. Conflicting messages create a feeling of push-pull between world and Spirit.

The world proclaims that we will have peace and happiness if only some person or some situation changes. Responsibility rests outside us. Spirit asks us to merge the power of our thoughts and motivations with its Divine power to create a peaceful and happy life. Responsibility rests within us.

The world regards judgment as a sign of maturity, strength and wisdom. Spirit warns us that judgments, based on past experience and distorted perceptions, are faulty and often wrong — whether or not we recognize our errors. Giving approval is a form of judgment, while seeking approval deprives us of inner peace. The world tells us to look out for number one and seek retribution for our grievances. Spiritual wisdom reminds us that God is love and that we are made in God's image and likeness. It's a paradox that love is our Divine nature and love is our greatest lesson to learn.

A full circle symbolizes love's wholeness. The Theater Garden with its circular design is a lovely space for reflection. It has stone benches and numerous plants with poetical names — prickly pear, showy sedum, and trifoliate-orange tree. In the early morning before the crowds arrive, I feel whole and serene within the confines of its circular stone wall. Its vibrant harmony fills me with love for all creation. Love is truly the fulcrum providing balance between world and Spirit.

The image of a seesaw from my childhood play comes to mind. If my partner was either too big or too small, I had a bumpy ride. If we were well matched in size, our ride was almost effortless. This seesaw image helps me remember the need to balance world and Spirit. It reminds me that I must love my Self, as well as others.

I learned about the power of love as a child, listening to stories in catechism class about the saints and martyrs. We were encouraged to follow their example and strive for unconditional love, the giving of love and expecting nothing in return. As I tackled this awesome task with childlike fervor, my grandmother — or Gay, as I named her — often came to mind as someone who loved me in this special way.

Memories of Gay come flooding back as I stroll through the Azalea Glen down by the large lake or pass by the lilac bushes near the main fountains. My mother, brother, and I moved into Gay's three-story home with its long, narrow back yard when my father went overseas during World War II. Each spring we had an Easter egg hunt. I always chose the pink azalea bush to search first. And Gay often cut clusters of purple and white lilac flowers to decorate our large dining room table. The azalea's beauty and the lilac's fragrance captured my attention as a child. They evoke such happiness many years later.

During the war I remember the air raid sirens and blackouts with shades drawn throughout our home. I sensed that, by reassuring me and soothing my fears, my grandmother also comforted herself. And then there was the trauma of first grade. I was the oldest. But I didn't want to leave my two brothers behind to have all the fun while I trudged off to school. Gay wiped my tears each morning with her apron and made me oatmeal in a double boiler—a breakfast I love even today. She frequently fed me grapefruit, keeping her thumb far up on the spoon so that it touched my lips. This habit annoyed me, but I didn't complain for fear of spoiling her loving gesture. Even as a small child, I knew intuitively that giving and receiving love are intertwined.

It's a paradox that giving and receiving are one. Different aspects of the same Life Force. With unconditional love, we strive to see the highest qualities in others and ourselves. By accepting our Sacred Self, we acknowledge that our true nature is one of abundance. The gifts of peace and joy are our spiritual birthright. We grow in love when we give these gifts to others. We deny ourselves when we withhold them.

In the world's view the giver loses and the taker benefits from this loss. Concern with scarcity as an approach to life makes giving a source of fear. Many of us have been wounded at some time or another by this lonely and isolated way of living. When we accept our own healing powers, we can choose instead to give compassionate healing to others. And we receive this gift in return from them.

Nature provides a wonderful window to observe the intricate process of giving and receiving. Down by the Italian Water Garden is the Beech Grove. These majestic trees can live up to two hundred years old and reach an imposing one hundred feet tall. They welcome the small visitors that come to enjoy their tasty nutlets. In turn, the trees rely on these birds and animals to spread their nuts to other areas for future growth.

But nature also reveals the possibility for imbalance in any relationship. Four giant sequoia trees sit high on the hill near the Eye of Water. Arborists put protective brass mesh around their huge trunks to keep squirrels from stripping away bark to line their nests. Otherwise the squirrels will endanger the health of these noble trees over time. Squirrels and giant sequoias have their own individual needs that they must meet to preserve their existence. They also must have a balanced relationship within the larger garden community. I sit on a bench nearby and ponder the delicate balance of give and take that any relationship requires. I think about my ongoing struggle to honor personal needs, as well as commitment to family, friends and the world community.

Perhaps the most vivid example I can offer is the complex relationship between the flowering plants and their pollinators. Flowers with showy shapes and brilliant colors act as scented billboards. They attract bees and butterflies to visit and reap their offerings of nectar and pollen. I appreciate this biological dance between plant and pollinator. I marvel at the life process taking place before my eyes. During garden walks I have the chance to know intimately nature's lessons on give and take.

We can practice so easily the lesson of giving and receiving in our daily lives. We can experience the results so quickly. And the most precious gifts we can offer one another are not material. Caring, appreciation and love enrich us beyond measure.

I make the intention in my morning prayers to offer each one I meet during the day a loving gift from the heart—a greeting, a smile or a silent blessing. I notice how swiftly my gifts return to me. I watch how I speak to others and remember that my words are either healing or harming. There is no in-between. I watch how I listen to others. I remember that the quality of my listening is often more important than the wisdom of my words. And I make a discovery. By filling each day with small acts of love and compassion, I am more inclined to be forgiving toward those who hurt me and hurt those I love.

It's a paradox that forgiveness heals your own mind, as well as the minds of those you forgive. It's a gift that brings peace to the giver and to the world. I've learned that forgiveness is an act of the will that sometimes does not come easily. I see an external world of pain and suffering—including Joe's with his cancer— and choose to forgive the thought that God wills this pain for others. I feel my own internal world of pain and suffering, especially now for my brother, and choose to forgive the thought that God wills this pain for me. I think about how I can see a hurtful act or situation from another person's perspective. I release my expectations for an apology or changed behavior. Forgiveness is a way of letting go.

I reflect on what it means to let go in nature. Bulbs planted deep in the soil of an earthly womb remind us that letting go is about darkness and mystery. But only through this dark process can bulbs grow and emerge as the springtime harbingers of new life. Rose bushes require pruning. Pruning is also a way of letting go. Pruning creates strength and new growth, but only if done wisely. Nature shows us the link between letting go and renewal. New birth demands reverence for darkness and mystery.

But so often we refuse to let go. We lack trust and fear uncertainty. We realize what no longer works for us but refuse to do our own pruning. Our spiritual growth lags. Sometimes the events in our lives help us with the letting go. They force us to face darkness and mystery. But they also build courage and strength for the journey ahead. Suffering and loss open us to appreciate what brings lasting joy in life. We're able to let go of the guilt and grievances—both real and imagined—that keep us in darkness. We choose instead to love and forgive others and ourselves. We choose to be instruments of divine grace, which is our calling.

Love and forgiveness offer us ways to participate as co-creators in the world's renewal. But first we must become comfortable with our inner power. We must find avenues for our fullest expression in a world where power has negative connotations.

Worldly power has come to mean imposing one's will over others and treating them with arrogance. Balance between world and Spirit does not require that we pit spiritual power against worldly power. Rather it asks us to live in awareness of who we really are. It asks us to act with a desire to influence others by recalling our connection with them. Despite the great forces for evil in the world and the overwhelming needs of many people, we must not lose hope. We must never doubt the power of one individual to create change.

Through chaos theory we have learned that a tiny influence can transform an entire system. A Chinese proverb beautifully captures this idea by stating that the power of a butterfly's wings can be felt on the other side of the world. Nature shows us that all creation is in constant flux. It is not a negative force, but a marvelous creative process of growth, decay and rebirth. Our complex world makes it difficult to predict the immediate future, much less the long-term outcome.

Our own interconnectedness makes it hard to predict the effects of our words and actions. How can we know what actually makes a difference? How can we understand our contributions in a larger sense? I find it humbling to consider that my words and actions as a teacher may influence my students for a long time to come.

Now when I see a butterfly in my garden walks, I pause to consider that the flutter of its fragile wings has more power than first meets the eye.

Butterfly power provides for the impossible. Anything can happen at any time. We adults become more rigid and bound up in the practical when faced with this thought. Children, however, are quite comfortable with the concept of the impossible. They easily understand that small things can bring about big effects.

During my last year of teaching I introduced the concept of butterfly power to my second grade students as a way of developing community in our classroom. Within sharing circle we discussed ways of making others happy through our words and actions. We wondered about the possibility of doing so without even knowing it.

Several days after our discussion, a distressed Ian came to me during dismissal—a time of organized chaos in most elementary classrooms. He was anxious because he had missed his science assignment from another teacher. I spied Anna sitting quietly, ready to go home. I asked her to help Ian with his concerns at the hall table.

The next day, her large brown eyes shining with delight, Anna listed the dozen or so persons she had made happy by helping Ian. We all clapped and took pleasure in Anna's happiness while she added twenty-three more people to her list.

I learned two powerful lessons from the fragile butterfly and the simple experience of an eight-year-old student. Small actions can have significance beyond our knowing. And when we give gladly to others, we always receive abundantly in return. Anna's story remains in my memory as I search for ways to explain butterfly power to others. It serves as a reminder that powerful effects often have small sources.

I love to watch the bees and butterflies visit the Buddleia alternifolia—the butterfly bushes—planted around the fountain on the main Flower Walk. For a brief period each spring small lavender flowers cover their branches. They fill the air with intoxicating fragrance and overwhelm my senses with their beauty.

Too quickly the flowering is finished. Gardeners prune away the branches and only a bare skeleton of the bush remains. The Buddleia alternifolia is not a pretty sight after it has been pruned. In fact the bush looks rather awkward and ugly. But new branches will grow again during the summer and on these branches next year's flowers will blossom. Nature offers another paradox for reflection. Pruning in one season provides for more abundant growth later on.

Pruning in our personal lives can take the form of problems and disappointments, setbacks and failures. We often see these events as unfortunate detours. And don't we feel awkward and ugly after we fail or endure an embarrassing setback? Only recently have I begun to appreciate the value of life's challenges. I now look for the seeds of opportunity embedded within them. But we need times of quiet reflection to understand the process of pruning and blossoming in our own lives. The Buddleia alternifolia reassures us that a loving Creator is still at work in the world.

This same Creator speaks to us through our hearts and releases us through our deepest feelings. We remember who we really are and why we are here on this earth. We must not allow ourselves to be fooled by appearances and swayed by the world's opinions. We must practice seeing with the eyes of Spirit.

Spiritual awareness reveals the paradox that love is our Divine nature and love is our greatest lesson to learn. Love is the common bond of our fallible humanity—the bond we share with our Creator. Love is the connection between the material and mystical worlds.

The world considers love a sentimental idea. Spirit regards love as the basis for all our words and actions. Love flows from the sacred Life Force within us all. It shows in our reverence and respect for others, all creation, and ourselves. Love is the fulcrum, providing balance between world and Spirit.

My search for harmony through the seasons in my lovely Gardens has come full circle. Each season offers its special images and lessons for me to ponder. I reflect on what I have learned during my garden walks and what these lessons mean for my life.

Reflections on a Journey

Now the seed of God is in us. The seed of a pear tree
grows into a pear tree.
The seed of a hazel tree grows into a hazel tree. And
the seed of God grows into God.

Meister Eckhart

I did not begin this journey with the dream of becoming a writer. I began with a desire—what I describe as a calling—to sort through my questions about life on paper. I needed a way to reflect on my search for balance between inner and outer worlds. I needed to grasp the lessons nature offered me on my garden walks. My writing is an expression of what I have learned until now. I'm ever evolving.

My search for balance is part of a legacy I've inherited from my father. I still feel a close bond with him, although he died too long ago. My dad was a man of strong convictions. He loved his family and his church and showed great passion for his work. Even as a child I understood these allegiances must have pulled him in difficult ways.

I watched his efforts to pay close attention to what I knew mattered most to him. It has taken many years for me to fathom this early understanding of my father. I now realize that my own search for life balance mirrors his.

I remember my dad as a caring man. Like him I've spent my life wanting to help others. How to balance inner needs with worldly service is the life lesson we both share. I don't know how my father felt about his life's balance or whether he thought much about it. I do feel my dad's presence now, most especially, as I write down what I've learned and share my lessons with others.

During years of quiet walks, I've found that nature helps me connect with Spirit — the Life Force of our Creator. My spiritual ideas evolve from intellect and intuition, world and Spirit. But how does one capture such knowing in words? The process of writing my truth unfolds slowly.

My brother Joe spoke of chipping away at his cancer. His imagery made me think of myself as a sculptor, chipping away at each chapter until a blueprint for balance took shape. Life lessons from nature emerged. I offer them for your reflection.

Appreciate the oneness and diversity of all creation.

Science tells the story of a dynamically alive universe. It describes nature as a complex, interconnected system that tends toward stasis. This tendency toward balance amid vibrant chaos may be the greatest mystery in all of nature. With awe we recognize our part in this wondrously varied yet unified system. Through nature we remember our mystical relationship with all creation.

Ancient spiritual teachings reveal the world as a sacred community shared by all living things. They teach us that a loving Life Force unites all creation as its Source. We learn to honor our uniqueness and the bond we share with others. We know that we are made in the image of our Creator. We remember our original blessing.

Nature awakens in me such awe for the wonder and mystery of our glorious universe and my own special place in it. As Hildegard of Bingen wrote, all creation reflects the Divine for me, "like a mirror, glistening and glittering with the Creator's image." I ask this loving Creator to help me find balance within myself and within society. I pray for the grace to live with compassion.

The world's wisdom traditions describe compassion as the fullest expression of a spiritual journey. They teach us that the opposite of love is not hate, but rather apathy—not caring. I've come to understand compassion as simple kindness toward all living things without exception. Our oneness requires compassionate action.

Natural and human worlds depend on oneness, diversity and shared purpose to maintain their balance. But harmony in the natural world includes not only the beauty of the earth's creative expression, but also its violence and decay. In our daily lives we witness the human potential for destruction as well as creation. It puzzles me that harmony embodies such disturbing aspects. Yet too much beauty exists for me to doubt an all-wise Creator. Life's blessings abound.

Appreciation of our oneness with all creation gives us hope. We are not alienated from one another. We are not alone. Appreciation for our diversity encourages trust, openness and inclusion. We are each unique and special. We each have value in our Creator's eyes. Appreciation for our shared purpose celebrates the necessary part each one plays in the world's harmony. We are citizens of the world. Knowledge of our unity and shared purpose requires an awareness of social and ecological issues.

The garden community serves as a metaphor for life. Who we are and what we say and do provide nutrients for the soil in which others grow. All members of the world community need nourishment and healing. But healing is not the end. It is a process that restores us to use our creative energies for the world's renewal. Through nature we can find a path to healing. Garden wisdom offers us ways to balance our inner needs with responsibility to serve in the world with generosity, forgiveness, and appreciation.

Connect with your Life Source only in the present.

In nature, past and future have no meaning. Life exists only in the present. We connect with Spirit—our breath, our Life Source, our true Self—only in the here and now.

We are infinite choice-makers. Each choice in the present moment is either toward Spirit or away from Spirit. Each choice determines our future. Always know your intention. We must make conscious choices toward love and away from fear. When we connect with Spirit, we are filled with compassion toward others and ourselves. When we go it alone, we are fearful. Strive to be aware of the present.

Living in the here and now requires practice and commitment. More than any other way, I have found that time in nature centers me and allows me to feel a connection with my Creator.

Any natural place that fulfills our need and reso-nates with our heart is the right place. Formal gardens or fields of wildflowers. Oceans, deserts or mountains. Flower boxes on a patio or flower pots on a windowsill. There is no particular place necessary to commune with the Divine through nature.

Before I take a walk in the gardens, I pause and ask for guidance from my Sacred Self: Help me to see as you see, hear as you hear, feel as you feel, know as you know. I let my surroundings wash over me—lush smells, vibrant colors, and serenades from the little birds that always make me smile. I touch the trunk of my tree friends, ask for a blessing and feel grounded and whole. Through these rituals I have discovered appreciation as a way of staying anchored and present throughout the day.

Full attention to the present moment is the most prayerful response we can make for the gift of life. It requires that we let go of our expectations and release our will to the Divine will. In return for our commitment we receive blessings beyond measure. We discover awareness of our deepest emotions, our heart's desires. We regain clarity about our purpose for being. And we maintain connection with the inner Source of our guidance and protection, power and strength.

Nurture your true Self during quiet times alone.

For me nature is a place of refuge and renewal. From nature I've learned that times of inner growth are necessary preparation for creative expression. Seeds receptive to nutrients from earth, rain and sun become the lovely blossoms of our gardens and flower boxes. Tasty nutlets forgotten by squirrels transform into the mighty oaks and beech trees that grow in our forests and woodlands and provide welcome shade in summer. Millions of bulbs planted each fall evolve into graceful daffodils blowing in the wind and announcing spring's arrival. Growth and change are part of a mysterious creative process that cannot be rushed either in nature or in our lives.

Creative expression is a mystery. It comes from the longings of the heart, not the logic of the mind. When I think too much about writing this book, I lose heart. Logic tells me I'm on a foolish venture—expecting to succeed in the publishing world.

I lack the impressive credentials of many authors I read. I struggle to translate my thoughts onto paper. And yet something from deep within compels me to continue.

My brother Joe's diagnosis with cancer forced me to confront this mysterious passion. I wondered what I would do with only a year to live. This stark question stripped away the non-essentials from my life and brought me closer to my soul's knowing. One desire surfaced and became clear. I would need to finish sharing my wisdom from the gardens.

Quiet times alone in nature can help prepare you for your own creative expression. But these times are more than just periods of stillness. They are opportunities to connect with the Life Force within and listen to the wisdom of your true Self. Times of solitude in nature restore your inner balance, make known your heartfelt desires, and release your deepest fears. You emerge prepared to share your gifts with the world. You go forth secure in your purpose and your trust in a Higher Power to help you always.

Trust that your life has meaning and purpose.

In both natural and human worlds, turmoil and disequilibrium are necessary parts of the creative cycle as life evolves into its more complete expression. When natural disaster strikes, nature adjusts and heals itself through its creative process. In times of human crisis and tragedy, we slowly heal and renew ourselves. But healing does not always occur. Death also happens.

During my Spirit walks I passed a newly transplanted Copper Beech tree. I began to notice withering leaves and knew it was struggling to survive, as arborists worked to save the young tree. One day I came by and it was gone. I remember how sad I was.

My brother Joe died of cancer at an early age despite the efforts of his doctors to save him and his own fierce determination to live. I remember Joe's acceptance of his death in every corner of my heart.

Early one morning Joe and I were sitting in the kitchen during one of my regular visits to offer him my love and support. He had tried to eat his soggy bowl of Cheerios for breakfast and found he was unable to swallow them. He said quietly, "This is not a good sign." We left the kitchen and went into the living room to sit. I grasped for ways to help Joe deal with yet another setback in his struggle with cancer's physical and emotional pain.

On this visit I had brought Joe a copy of *The Problem of Pain*, by C. S. Lewis. Our Aunt Bee had used this book's wisdom to help her endure many years of suffering with rheumatoid arthritis. I knew Joe felt a close bond with Aunt Bee. We began to discuss the age-old dilemma of why good people suffer and how they should respond to this suffering. I shared with Joe that C. S. Lewis had concluded "Thy will be done" was the necessary response. Joe smiled and said, "I like that." He rested his head against the high back chair and repeated softly three times: "I accept. I accept. I accept." Stillness came over him as I sat transfixed by the power of his words. Three days later my brother died a peaceful death.

Joe had found the courage to accept Divine will in his life and I had received the grace to witness his act of faith. "Thy will be done" is a central tenet of human existence, yet we are so afraid to trust Divine purpose. Letting go is at the heart of any spiritual journey, yet we cling with such tenacity to our petty wills and our need for control. We wrestle in vain with the question, "Why?" We forget that change and mystery are present in nature and present in our lives. They are an integral part of all growth, along with timing and resilience.

Learn first to accept and appreciate life as it is. Do the best that you can in any given situation and then let go. Trust that your Sacred Self will work through you for the highest good. Letting go is an act of faith.

Learn to appreciate the sunshine and shadows that reside in each of us, in our relationships, and in life itself. Cycles of good and difficult times occur in both natural and human worlds. Trust that a loving Creator knows and cares for the needs of every living thing. As our trust grows, so does our inner peace. With trust comes healing.

Know that loving acts for others enrich you as well.

Bees and butterflies pollinate the lovely flowers they visit and in return receive offerings of nectar and pollen. Squirrels enjoy nutlets from the beech trees and help spread them for future growth. We can observe in nature the powerful lesson that giving and receiving are one—both aspects of the same Life Force. This loving Life Force is the common bond we share with each other and the source for our creative expression in the world. Love is the fulcrum, providing balance between world and Spirit.

Through nature I can understand more fully the awesome power of Divine love. When I gaze at a mighty oak tree, I find it difficult to grasp that a small acorn contains everything necessary for its growth. I stand beneath the lofty branches and ask for grace to become who I really am—to accept that I have all I need to accomplish my purpose for living. But I understand that the oak's growth from a small acorn to a majestic tree has its own rhythm that can't be rushed.

Just as nature has certain rhythms, so also does love. The growth process of a tiny seed requires that its needs be met at every stage. Sometimes darkness is necessary and sometimes light. Like the tiny seed, our own growth process requires that we be patient and loving with ourselves. Sometimes we need to give and receive hugs. Sometimes we just need space. But always, a loving Life Force supports us as we claim our inner power with humility and reach out to others with love.

Quiet time in nature opens my heart and fills it with appreciation and compassion. And yet I struggle often to balance my personal needs with my desire to contribute to the world's renewal. I embody the paradox I write about: Love is our divine nature and love is our greatest lesson to learn. I become frustrated and discouraged that I keep repeating the same mistakes.

I was strolling in Longwood Gardens one day pondering these thoughts when I became acquainted with my little Princess tree friend. It was growing in the newly restored Paulownia Allee. The sign told me that gardeners would cut back a young tree with a crooked trunk in order to force a new straight leader to grow from the base. The new leader will quickly form a new main trunk. I noticed this particular tree because its small trunk was beginning to grow crooked.

I'd walk by my young tree friend and smile as I warned it to straighten up or risk being whacked. But it needed to grow the hard way—as I often do—and was cut back several times until a straight trunk grew. The little Princess tree reminds me that we keep having the same life lessons return to us until we get them straight. We keep revisiting the same truths throughout our lives until we begin to understand them.

Afterword: Life Balance and Joy

In these pages I have filtered old truths through the lens of my experience and my awareness of nature's wisdom. I wrote this book to find out who I am, what I know, and what I feel. The blueprint for balance that evolved is my vision—my response to the dilemma of how to live in the world with Spirit. If my wisdom from the gardens resonates in your heart, then I am thankful. I offer it to you as a blessing and a guide for your own spiritual search.

Learning from Spirit takes discipline and willingness to create our own sacred space in the midst of a frenetic world. Discipline comes from the same root as disciple—a follower—one who desires to learn. If we want to connect with Spirit, then we must pay attention and show our commitment.

I believe that the world's survival depends on a deep connection to Spirit. With Spirit we celebrate our oneness and diversity and live with care for the natural world and all human beings. In Spirit we savor each present moment and sanctify even our smallest acts, from making a cup of tea to taking out the garbage. Through Spirit we find our sense of purpose and share our gifts to restore the world's harmony.

Commitment to your soul's purpose changes your life forever. I will not say that it's easy, but it always provides healing and brings joy. You may find your life seems to fall apart at first, as mine did. But I now understand those experiences were necessary. They reset my energies and my life course in a more comfortable direction for my soul growth. Through them I found the courage to follow my dreams with conviction and excitement, wondering where they will lead me. Daily I ask for Spirit guidance: Help me to feel what is true and know what to do next. A response always comes, but not always in a way I expect.

It is my desire to show that Spirit belongs in everyday life and not just in the realm of saints and mystics. I intend my blueprint for balance as a plan to help busy people wanting to live with Spirit in the world. But how do we remain whole in the midst of life's pushes and pulls? My garden lessons have taught me the value of keeping things simple.

Each morning make your intention to serve as a co-creator with Spirit to accomplish your purpose for being on earth. Keep your attention on the present. Live with appreciation and belief in the power of your true Self. Find ways to nurture your dreams. Being in the present does not take away the desires of your heart. They come from Spirit. Make time for solitude and inner growth. Your creative expression will blossom because of it. Spend time in nature to strengthen your understanding of these lessons. And make this practice simple too. My mother always kept an African violet on her kitchen windowsill. Small acts also renew us.

A search for balance between world and Spirit lured me into the gardens. I was running on empty. I felt parched and dry inside. My wisdom from the gardens has taught me to create, not a dualism between world and Spirit, but rather a blending. It has revitalized me with new joy and zest for life. But this is only a beginning.

I am still learning.